LEVEL 3

The Canterville Ghost
and Other Stories

Adapted by

Pam Davies

Richmond READERS

Richmond READERS

LEVEL 1

(500 headwords)

Maria's Dilemma
Oscar
Jack's Game
The Boy from Yesterday
The Black Mountain

LEVEL 2

(800 headwords)

Jason Causes Chaos
Craigen Castle Mystery
The Road through the Hills and Other Stories
Where's Mauriac?
Saturday Storm

LEVEL 3

(1200 headwords)

A Trip to the Stars
Dr Jekyll and Mr Hyde
The Canterville Ghost and Other Stories
Cold Feet
Frankenstein

LEVEL 4

(1800 headwords)

A Trip to London
Dracula
Jane Eyre
The Adventures of Tom Sawyer
Sense and Sensibility

LEVEL 5

(2600+ headwords)

Steve Jobs: the man behind Apple
Elizabeth II The Diamond Queen

The Canterville Ghost and Other Stories

'You'll be sorry you bought the house,' people told Mr Hiram B. Otis.' 'Everyone knows that a ghost lives there.' But the Otises are a modern American family, and they don't believe in ghosts.

Pam Davies studied history at university and is married to a geologist. They have two sons. She taught British history and English during her husband's work in foreign countries. Now, she has given up teaching and is enjoying more time for writing, gardening and walking.

LEVEL 3

2

Introduction

Oscar Wilde

Oscar Wilde was born in Dublin in 1854. His father was a well-known Irish doctor and his mother was a poet, writing under the pseudonym 'Speranza'.

After an early education in Ireland, Wilde went to Oxford University where he was a brilliant student. He also became well known as someone who had little respect for the conventions of the age. Unlike other men of his class, he hated sport. Instead, he was more interested in collecting beautiful objects to fill his rooms. At a time when gentlemen were always formally dressed, Wilde wore his hair long and appeared in public in unusual clothes, carrying a flower in his hand. Some people found such behaviour hard to tolerate. On one occasion, an angry group of students threw him into the river.

On leaving Oxford, Wilde went to London where he soon became famous for his clever wit* and brilliant conversation. He spent his time writing and giving talks in both England and America.

In 1884, Wilde married Constance Lloyd, the daughter of an Irish lawyer, and they had two sons. At this time Wilde found regular work on a popular magazine. In 1888, he published a collection of children's stories that he had written for his sons. They were followed in 1891 by another collection of stories, including the ones in this book.

But Wilde's greatest success came with the plays he wrote for the London theatre over the next five years. *Lady Windermere's Fan* and *The Importance of Being Earnest* were the most famous of these and they are still popular today. He wrote only one novel, *The Picture of Dorian Gray,* which was published in 1891.

Unfortunately, not all the attention Wilde attracted was favourable. He had many enemies who disliked his colourful and unconventional way of life, and said ugly things about him. Eventually, he used the law to fight one of them, but lost his case. When he was sent to prison for his unconventional behaviour, his life was destroyed.

Wilde chose to spend his last years abroad. In 1898, his wife died, and Wilde himself died in Paris in 1900.

Society in the late nineteenth century

In *The Sphinx** *without a Secret* and *The Model** *Millionaire,* Oscar Wilde writes about the lives of rich people in London's high society at the end of the nineteenth century. Such people did not usually need to work for money, although some did follow professions, for example in the army or in government. Their money usually came from houses and land passed down through families. The men spent much of their time riding, shooting and fishing or watching the great seasonal sporting events like horse races. An important part of an upper class man's life when he was in London, was his club. Gentlemen's clubs were like a second home, especially for unmarried men. They were comfortable places where men could go to enjoy serious conversation, to have a meal, to play a game of cards or just to smoke and drink away from the control of women.

Women's lives were very narrow. Upper class women spent a lot of time giving dinner parties and formal dances in the evenings. It was important to have the most brilliant guests and the finest food. In the afternoons, they would dress in the most fashionable clothes and drive in the parks or visit their friends.

Relations between the sexes were very formal. Rules of behaviour had to be obeyed. An unmarried girl had to guard her good name carefully or she would never get a husband. A married woman could not be too friendly with a man who was not her husband or even be alone with one. Breaking these rules or even behaving suspiciously with the opposite sex could destroy a woman's life. Once her good name was gone, she lost her position in society forever.

Wilde often laughed gently at the extreme attitudes of the English upper class. In *The Canterville Ghost,* he enjoys comparing the attitudes of the American Otis family with traditional English upper-class values. The Otis family respect people for being independent and for their success as individuals. The English upper class, on the other hand, might respect people for being born into a certain family or class. Wilde clearly feels that the American way is a breath of fresh air.

The Canterville Ghost

Author's note

Although *The Canterville Ghost* is a comic story, it has poetic touches. Birds and plants are used symbolically within the story. Some of them are illustrated here.

nightingale
(Luscinia megarhynchos)

barn owl
(Tyto alba)

rook
(Corvus frugilegus)

cock
(Gallus domesticus)

almond tree
(Prunus dulcis)

white hemlock
(Conium maculatum)

CHAPTER I 3

Bloodstain on the Floor*

'You'll be sorry you bought the house,' people told Mr Hiram B. Otis. 'Everyone knows that a ghost* lives in it.'

Mr Otis was a rich American who had just bought a fine, old house called Canterville Chase. It had been the country home of Lord• Canterville, who had been completely honest with Mr Otis about his reasons for selling it.

'We haven't liked living in the place ourselves since an old aunt of mine was terribly frightened by the ghost,' Lord Canterville told Mr Otis. 'Two skeleton* hands touched her as she was dressing for dinner. And I must tell you, Mr Otis, that several other members of my family have also seen it. My wife herself cannot sleep at night because of the noises in the library*...'

'I'll take the furniture and the ghost, Sir,' answered Mr Otis. 'I come from a modern country where money can buy anything. If there's a ghost here, I'll send it to America. Back home*, they'll pay to see it!'

• *In English high society, a lord, like Lord Canterville, comes below a duke. A duke, like the Duke of Cheshire who appears later in the story, is second in social position only to the King or Queen.*

'Two skeleton hands touched her as she was dressing for dinner.'

'It's certainly here,' said Lord Canterville. 'The ghost has been well known for three hundred years. It always appears before the death of anyone in the family.'

'So does the family doctor,' replied Mr Otis. 'There are no ghosts, Sir. The laws of nature can't be broken, not even for an English lord!'

Lord Canterville did not quite understand the American's last words. Like most Americans, Mr Otis was a practical man. He respected individual effort. He respected the power of money and those who earned it. The high social position of families like the Cantervilles meant nothing to him. Lord Canterville, on the other hand, had been born to the money and social position of the English upper class. He could not imagine anything different.

'If you don't mind a ghost in the house,' he said, 'then that's all right. But remember that I warned you.'

A few weeks later, the sale was completed and Mr Otis took his family down to Canterville Chase.

Mrs Otis was a good-looking, energetic woman in her middle age. Washington Otis, her eldest son, was an attractive young man with fair hair and a talent for dancing. He worked for Pinkerton's Chemical Company. They invented new and wonderful medicines, and things to help with cleaning the house.

Miss Virginia Otis came next. She was a lovely girl of fifteen with large blue eyes. Virginia was as energetic as her mother. She loved horse riding. She had recently won a horse race against some very good riders. One of them was the young Duke of Cheshire, who had at once fallen in love with her. After Virginia came the twins*– twin boys, who were usually called the 'Stars and

Stripes•' because they were often beaten for their bad behaviour.

Canterville Chase was seven miles* from the nearest town so Mr Otis had ordered a carriage to meet them at the railway station. They were all happy as they started their drive. It was a sunny July evening. The air was soft and sweet with the smells of summer. Little animals ran about busily in the grass and the sound of birds could be heard in the trees. But when the carriage turned towards Canterville Chase, dark clouds filled the sky. Everything suddenly became quiet. A crowd of large rooks flew silently over the heads of the Otis family. Before the Otises reached the house, it started to rain heavily.

On the steps in front of the big house, an old woman was waiting. She was wearing a black dress with a white cap* on her head. This was Mrs Umney, who had been Lady Canterville's housekeeper*. Mrs Otis had agreed to let her stay in the job.

'I hope you will all be very happy in Canterville Chase,' said Mrs Umney.

They followed her into the library of the house. It was a long, low room with walls of dark wood. At the far end, there was a beautiful window of coloured glass. Tea was all ready for them on a small table. They sat down and looked round, while Mrs Umney filled their tea cups.

Mrs Otis suddenly noticed a large, red stain* on the floor near the fireplace. She pointed at it. 'What's this, Mrs Umney? I don't like dirty floors in my house!'

'That's blood, Madam,' said the housekeeper in a low,

• *The 'Stars and Stripes' is the affectionate name given to the American flag. The twins get* stripes *on their backs and see* stars *before their eyes when they are beaten.*

But when the carriage turned towards Canterville Chase, dark clouds filled the sky.

mysterious voice. 'Blood has always marked the floor in this room.'

'How horrible,' said Mrs Otis. 'I don't like bloodstains in my sitting room. You must clean it at once, Mrs Umney.'

The old woman smiled and answered in the same low, mysterious voice. 'It's the blood of Lady Eleanore de Canterville. She was murdered here in 1575 by her husband, Sir Simon de Canterville. Sir Simon lived for another nine years. Then he mysteriously disappeared. His body has never been found, but his unhappy ghost still haunts* the house. The bloodstain has been much admired by tourists ... It can't be washed away.'

'Of course it can!' said Washington Otis, who was just as practical as his father. In his business, there was strong competition, and he had learned that nothing was impossible for a good salesman. 'Pinkerton's Detergent will do it at once.' He took a little black bottle out of his pocket. Before the surprised housekeeper could stop him, Washington got down on the floor. He worked on the stain for a few moments and it soon disappeared.

'I knew Pinkerton's would do it,' he said. He looked round at his admiring family. At that moment, bright lightning* lit up the room, followed by a loud crash of thunder*. They all jumped up from their chairs and Mrs Umney fell down on the floor, unconscious.

Mr Otis calmly lit a cigarette. 'What terrible weather you have in England,' he said to the unconscious woman.

Mrs Umney recovered* in a few minutes, but she was still very upset. She warned Mr Otis to be careful. 'Trouble is coming to this house, Sir,' she said. 'I've seen things here that have made my hair stand up on my head!

'I knew Pinkerton's would do it,' he said.

There have been many nights when I haven't been able to close my eyes in sleep...'

'We don't believe in ghosts,' Mr Otis told her firmly. 'But we'll pay you more money if you agree to stay with us.' This kind promise pleased the old woman. She let Virginia lead her away to her own room for a rest.

4

CHAPTER 2

A Shock for the Ghost

The storm continued all that night, but nothing else unusual happened. At breakfast the next morning, however, the Otis family found that the terrible bloodstain on the floor had reappeared.

'I don't think it's the fault of Pinkerton's Detergent,' said Washington. 'Pinkerton's cleans everything else. It must be the work of the ghost.'

He cleaned the stain for the second time. But on the second morning, it was back. That night the library was locked and Mr Otis himself kept the key in his pocket. But on the third morning the stain was back.

The whole family were now quite interested. Mr Otis began to think that his opinions about ghosts had been wrong. Washington Otis wrote a long letter to the Pinkerton Chemical Company on the subject of difficult stains. And Mrs Otis decided to join a society for people who wanted to learn about ghosts.

In America, she had belonged to a variety of societies.

She thought she was a very good organiser, and she enjoyed managing groups of people. But she had been disappointed to find that her English neighbours did not seem to need her talents.

The fourth day was warm and sunny. The family went out for a drive and did not return until nine o'clock. They had a light supper and talked about many different things. But nobody mentioned ghosts. No thought of ghosts entered their heads. At eleven o'clock, they went to bed and by half past eleven all lights were out.

Some time later, Mr Otis was woken up by a strange noise outside his room. It was the sound of metal on stone, and it was coming nearer with every minute. Mr Otis got up and calmly looked at his watch. It was exactly one o'clock. The strange noise continued and now he could also hear the sound of footsteps*. He put on his shoes, took a small glass bottle out of his case and opened the door.

A terrible old man was standing in front of him in the bright moonlight. His eyes were as red as fire. Long, dirty grey hair fell down his back. His clothes were very old and full of holes. There were heavy chains on his legs and arms.

'My dear Sir,' said Mr Otis, 'let me give you some oil for those chains. They make a terrible noise. Here is a small bottle of Pinkerton's Best Lubricating Oil. I expect you've heard of it. I'm told that it's very effective. I'll leave it here for you.' He put the small bottle down on the floor. 'There's plenty more if you need it,' he said kindly, and went back to bed.

For a moment, the Canterville ghost was too shocked to move. Then he threw the little bottle violently against the wall. He was lit by a horrible green light as he ran

'My dear Sir,' said Mr Otis, 'Let me give you some oil for those chains.'

through the house. His terrible screams could be heard everywhere.

When he reached the top of some wooden stairs, a door opened. Two small figures dressed in white appeared. A large pillow* was thrown at his head! He decided to escape at once, and disappeared through the nearest wall. The house became quiet.

The ghost was breathing heavily when he reached his own secret little room. It was in a part of the house that was not used much. He sat down and began to think about his new situation. For three hundred years people had shown him the greatest respect. Frightening people had been great fun!

He thought of the old French lady, Madame de Tremouillac. She had woken up one morning to see a skeleton reading her diary. For years after that, she had suffered from nervous illness. Then there was the butler* who drank too much, and shot himself in the kitchen because he saw a green hand opening the window. And the beautiful Lady Stutfield, who always had to cover her neck because of the five fingermarks burnt onto her white skin...

Now, after centuries of success, some horrible modern Americans had arrived. They offered him Pinkerton's Lubricating Oil and threw pillows at his head. He could not tolerate it. No other ghost in history had suffered such humiliation*. He must think of ways to make them pay for their terrible behaviour.

5 CHAPTER 3

The Ghost Gets Upset

The next morning, the Otis family discussed the ghost at breakfast. Mr Otis was a little angry that the ghost had not accepted his present.

'I don't wish to cause the ghost any personal injury,' he said, 'and I don't think it's polite to throw pillows at him.' The twins shouted with laughter. 'But if he won't use Pinkerton's Lubricating Oil,' continued Mr Otis, 'we shall have to take his chains from him. It's quite impossible to sleep with all that noise outside the bedrooms.'

For the rest of the week, they were free from trouble. The only excitement was the bloodstain on the library floor. It continued to reappear regularly each morning, although the windows and door were always locked at night. Some mornings it was dark red, others it was deep blue and once it was bright green ... These changes made the family laugh. Every evening they tried to guess what the next day's colour would be.

The only person who did not enjoy the joke was Virginia. For some reason, she was always upset by the bloodstain. On the morning when it was bright green, she even cried a little.

The ghost appeared for the second time on Sunday night. Soon after they had all gone to bed, there was a heavy crash from below. Mr Otis, Washington and the twins ran down and found a large suit of old armour* on the floor. The Canterville ghost was sitting in a chair with an expression of great pain on his face. The twins immediately began to throw pieces of firewood at him.

The Canterville ghost was sitting in a chair with an expression of great pain on his face.

They had practised a lot at school where they threw things at their teacher. Mr Otis pointed a gun at the ghost and told him to put his hands up.

The ghost gave a wild scream of anger, put out all the lights and ran up the stairs. He turned at the top and let out a great shout of his most horrible laughter. On more than one occasion, this had been very effective.

A door opened behind him and Mrs Otis came out with a large bottle of medicine in her hand. 'You sound very unwell,' she said. 'I've brought you some of Pinkerton's Medicine for All Known Illnesses. It's very good for a bad stomach. I'm sure it will soon make you feel better.'

The ghost looked at her angrily and started to turn himself into a large black dog. This never failed to cause terror. In fact, Lord Canterville's uncle had gone mad after seeing it. But then the ghost heard the approaching footsteps of the twins and changed his mind. Instead, he gave one last angry scream ... and disappeared.

Back in his own room, the ghost was extremely unhappy. The disrespectful behaviour of the twins and Mrs Otis's offer of practical help had upset him. It was not the right way to act towards a real ghost. But most of all he was angry because he had not been able to wear the suit of armour. A ghostly figure in armour would excite even modern Americans, he thought. And it was his own armour. It had helped him to win competitions. Queen Elizabeth I herself had sent him her congratulations. But when he had tried to put it on tonight, it had been too heavy for him. He had fallen on the stone floor and hurt both legs quite badly.

For some days, the ghost was very ill and only left his room to take care of the bloodstain in the library.

CHAPTER 4 6

The Ghostly Plan

When he felt better, he decided to try again to frighten the American family. This time, he made very careful preparations.

First, he decided what clothes to wear. He chose a large hat with a red feather. Then he put a white shroud* round himself. Finally, he picked up a large, bloodstained knife. In the evening a violent storm broke. A strong wind blew noisily through the old house. The ghost was pleased. It was just the kind of weather he loved.

He went through his plan of action. 'I will go to Washington Otis's room first and make noises at the foot of his bed. Then I will push the knife into myself three times. Slow, sad music will play. When the young man is helpless with terror, I will go to the parents' room. I will put a thin, ice-cold hand on Mrs Otis's head and say awful things in a low, frightening voice to Mr Otis.' The ghost was not quite so certain about his plans for Virginia. She was gentle and pretty, and she had never tried to hurt him. 'A few alarming noises from inside the cupboard in her room will be enough,' he thought.

But he certainly intended to frighten the terrible twins. 'First, I will sit on them heavily so that they cannot breathe. Then I will appear in the form of a dead body, lit by a horrible green light...'

He chose a large hat with a red feather. Then he put a white shroud round himself.

At half past ten, he heard the family going to bed. For some time there were screams of laughter from the twins' room. But at a quarter past eleven all was quiet and at midnight, the ghost left his room. A barn owl called softly from a tree outside the window. The wind cried like a lost child through the empty rooms of the house. But the Otis family slept peacefully, unconscious of the coming danger.

The ghost moved quietly through the darkness of the sleeping house. A cruel smile touched his dry, old mouth. He held his bloody knife high in the air. He felt so powerful! He was beginning to enjoy himself.

Still smiling, he turned the corner to reach Washington's room. He stopped with a shout of terror! Directly in front of him stood a terrible, ghostly figure. It was like a madman's worst dream. The large, round head was white and hairless. The fat face was smiling horribly. A strange red fire lit up its eyes and mouth. The awful figure was wearing a white shroud, very like his own.

There was a notice on the cloth in strange, old writing. In its right hand, the figure held a large, sharp knife.

The Canterville ghost had never before seen anything like this! He was extremely frightened. He gave the awful thing one last look. Then he ran back to his own room, where he hid under the bed until morning.

Daylight helped him to feel braver so he decided to return to the same place and speak to the other ghost. But he found the stranger on the floor. The light had gone from its eyes and the knife had dropped from its hand. When he tried to lift it up, he had a terrible shock. The head fell off! He looked down. He was holding a white bed sheet, a long kitchen brush and a meat knife. A large pumpkin was lying on the floor. The ghost could not understand what had happened. Nervously, he looked at the notice on the white cloth and read these words:

The Otis Ghost.
'The Only True and Original
Otis Ghost! Take care!
All other ghosts are false.'

Then he suddenly understood! Somebody was laughing at him. An angry look came into his eyes. He lifted his thin, old hands above his head and made a great promise. 'When the cock crows* twice, horrible things will happen here. Murder will walk in this house on silent feet!'

He had just said these awful words when a cock crowed. The ghost laughed a long, low laugh ... and waited. Hour after hour he waited, but for some strange reason the bird did not crow again.

Finally, at half past seven, he went back to his room. 'If I ever meet that bird,' he told himself, 'I'll cut off its head!'

Somebody was laughing at him.

7

CHAPTER 5
Headless Rupert

The next day, the ghost felt very weak and tired. The terrible excitement of the last four weeks was beginning to have its effect. He was extremely nervous, and jumped at the least little noise. For five days, he stayed in his room. Finally, he decided to stop putting the bloodstain on the library floor. It did not frighten the Otis family. They were obviously people of very low class who were only interested in material things. His work was wasted on them.

But his ghostly appearances were a different matter. They had happened for three hundred years and he could not really change them. On the first and third Wednesdays in every month, he had always appeared at the large north window of the library. There, he screamed his awful screams. He was certainly not going to stop doing that.

The Canterville ghost had been a very bad man, but some things were still important to him. He had to continue to play his ghostly part in the life of Canterville Chase.

For the next three weeks, between midnight and three o'clock, he walked about as usual. But he was careful to be very quiet. He took off his boots and walked as lightly as possible on the floors. He also used Pinkerton's Lubricating Oil on his noisy chains. He had not wanted to use it. But one evening at dinner time, he had gone to Mr Otis's room and had taken the little black bottle. He had to agree that it was very effective.

But he was still not left in peace. The twins played

practical jokes on him every night. Things were put in his way so that he would fall over them in the dark. One night, he had a very serious fall. The boys had put butter* at the top of some stairs ... The ghost could no longer be patient.

For the last time, he must try to make the Otis family understand how important he was.

After some deep thought, he decided to appear in the form of 'Headless Rupert'. This was one of his favourite characters. Its last appearance had been most satisfying. He had so frightened pretty little Lady Barbara in 1793 that she had refused to marry Lord Canterville's grandfather.

'I will never marry into the family that has such a horrible ghost!' she said. And six months later, she died of a broken heart. The ghost smiled happily at the memory.

It took him a long time to prepare himself for the Rupert character because it was difficult to dress himself without his head. But finally, he was ready. He was quite pleased with himself when he looked in the mirror. The riding boots were a little too big and he could not find the right hat. But he thought his general appearance was excellent.

At a quarter past one, he went silently on his way to the twins' room. It was called the 'Blue Room' because of the colour of the wallpaper. The door was not completely shut. The ghost wanted to make a really effective entrance so he suddenly pushed the door wide open. A large container of water fell down from the top of the door. The container flew past his shoulder and he was completely covered in ice-cold water!

Screams of laughter came from the bed. The ghost was

A large container of water fell down from the top of the door.

terribly shocked. He quickly ran back to his room. The next day he was very ill.

'It's a good thing that I didn't take my head with me,' he said to himself. 'I might feel even worse.'

CHAPTER 6 8

Terror in the Library

The ghost now realised that he could never frighten the American family. He continued his nightly walks about the house, but he wore his softest shoes. He carried a small gun to protect himself from an attack by the twins.

Finally, two weeks later, the worst thing happened. The ghost had gone down to the library. He wanted to examine the condition of the bloodstain. He felt safe enough. It was past two o'clock in the morning and no one was moving. He looked at the two new photographs of Mr and Mrs Otis on the wall. They were there in place of the Canterville family portraits*. 'Horrible people!' said the ghost to himself. 'No history or tradition...'

Suddenly, two figures jumped at him from a dark corner. They put their arms above their heads and screamed into his ear, 'BOO!' The ghost ran to the stairs in terror, but Washington Otis was waiting for him. He was holding a garden hosepipe* ... With enemies on all sides, the ghost had to escape through the fireplace. Fortunately, the fire was not lit. But the ghost reached his own room in a very dirty and unhappy condition.

After this, the ghost was never again seen at night. The

twins waited for him on several occasions, but he did not appear. His feelings were very deeply hurt. But the Otis family soon forgot him and became interested in other things.

Mrs Otis successfully organised a large garden party. The local people talked about it for weeks. Virginia rode about the country on her horse with the young Duke of Cheshire. He was spending a holiday at Canterville Chase. The family believed that the ghost had gone away. Mr Otis wrote to tell Lord Canterville, who was very pleased at the news.

But the Otises were wrong. The ghost had not gone away. Although he now felt almost permanently ill, the ghost was not ready to leave Canterville Chase. He was interested in the family's young guest. The Duke of Cheshire's uncle had once tried to play cards with the Canterville ghost. The next morning he had been found helpless on the library floor. He never spoke another word. The ghost wanted to show that he still had the same power and influence. He planned to appear in the Duke's bedroom in one of his most terrible forms. But at the last moment, terror of the twins kept him in his room. The young Duke slept untroubled in his bed and dreamed of Virginia.

CHAPTER 7

9

A Young Girl's Tears

A few days later, Virginia and the Duke went out as usual. Unfortunately, Virginia fell off her horse and came home with holes in her riding dress. She did not want her family to see her. 'The twins will make jokes and Mother will worry,' she said to herself. So she went to her room by the back stairs.

On the way, she passed a little room she had not seen before. The door was open and she looked inside. She was surprised to see the Canterville ghost! He was sitting on his bed with his head in his hands. He looked very unhappy.

At first, Virginia wanted to run away from the ghost. Then she felt sorry for him. She decided she must try to help. The ghost did not notice her until she spoke.

'I'm so sorry for you,' she said. 'But my little brothers are going back to school tomorrow. After that, if you behave well, no one will trouble you.'

The ghost looked at the pretty girl who had spoken. 'I can't behave well,' he answered in surprise. 'It's a stupid idea. I have to walk about at night and scream through keyholes. I have to make a noise with my chains. I exist for that reason. It's a ghost's job.'

'It's no reason at all,' replied Virginia, firmly. 'You know you've been very bad, don't you? Mrs Umney told us. You killed your wife.'

'Yes ... yes, I did,' said the ghost. 'But that was just family business. It affected no one else.'

'It's very wrong to kill anyone,' said Virginia.

She decided she must try to help.

'What do you know about it?' said the ghost impatiently. 'My wife was very ugly. She didn't take care of my clothes and she couldn't cook. After her death, her brothers locked me up and gave me no food. It wasn't very nice of them. I starved* to death.'

'Starved to death?' repeated Virginia. 'Oh, Mr Ghost ... I mean, Sir Simon, are you hungry? I have a sandwich in my pocket. Would you like it?'

'No, thank you. I never eat anything now. But you're a very kind girl. You're much nicer than the rest of your family. They are very common*, unkind people.'

'Stop!' said Virginia. 'You have faults, too. You aren't very honest. You took colours from my paintbox for that bloodstain in the library, didn't you? First you took all the reds, then the blues and greens. I didn't tell anyone, but you were very stupid. Who has ever seen green blood?'

'Well, what could I do?' said the ghost weakly. 'I couldn't get any real blood. It's difficult these days. Your brother started it all, anyway, with his Pinkerton's Detergent. After all, it was my bloodstain. So I thought I could use your paints to put it back ... And colour is a matter of opinion. The Cantervilles have always had blue blood, of course. But I know you Americans don't appreciate these things.'

'You know nothing about it,' said Virginia. 'Why don't you go to America and learn something? You'll be a great success in New York. I know lots of people who would pay a hundred thousand dollars to have a grandfather, and even more to have a family ghost.'

'If the people are all like your family, I wouldn't like America.'

'Goodbye. I'll go and ask Father to give the twins another week's holiday.' She turned towards the door.

'Please don't go, Miss Virginia,' the ghost said. 'I'm so lonely and unhappy. I don't know what to do. I want to go to sleep and I can't.'

'Just go to bed and turn off the light,' Virginia suggested. 'Sometimes it's difficult to stay awake - in church, for example - but even babies can go to sleep.'

'I haven't slept for three hundred years,' said the ghost sadly. Virginia's beautiful blue eyes opened wide. 'For three hundred years, I haven't slept,' the ghost repeated. 'And I'm so tired.'

Virginia looked very serious. Her eyes were wet. She went towards him and knelt down on the floor at his side.

'Poor, poor ghost,' she said softly. 'Have you no place where you can sleep?'

He answered in a low, dreamy voice. 'Far away, beyond the woods, there's a little garden. White hemlock grows there. The nightingale sings all night, while the cold moon looks down. A great, dark tree holds out its old arms over the quiet sleepers...'

Virginia hid her face in her hands. 'You mean the Garden of Death,' she said.

'Yes, Death. Death must be so beautiful ... so quiet and peaceful. No yesterday ... no tomorrow. You can help me, Miss Virginia. You can open the door of Death's house for me because you are in love. Love is always with you. And Love is stronger than Death.'

Virginia felt suddenly cold. It was like a terrible dream. For a few moments, there was silence.

Then the ghost spoke again. 'Have you ever read the writing on the library window?'

'Quick! Quick, or it will be too late,' he said.

'Oh, often,' said the girl. 'I know it quite well. It's painted in strange, black letters. It says that peace will come to Canterville with the help of a young girl's tears. And then, the dead almond tree in the garden will flower again ... I don't know what it means.'

'It means that you must cry for me...' said the ghost, 'for all the bad things I have done, because I cannot cry. If you are sweet and good and gentle, Death will be kind. Go to Death for me. You will see fearful forms in the darkness, but you needn't be afraid. Cruel voices will speak in your ear, but they won't hurt you.'

Virginia's face was white, but her eyes were bright and she spoke in a firm voice. 'I'm not afraid,' she said. 'I'll go to Death and ask him to be kind to you.'

The ghost stood up, took her hand and kissed it. His fingers were as cold as ice and his mouth burned her skin like fire. He led Virginia across the room. She seemed to hear voices crying, 'Go back, Virginia! Go back!' But the ghost held her hand firmly and she refused to listen.

When they reached the opposite wall of the room, the ghost said something quickly in a low voice. Virginia saw the wall slowly disappear. A great, black hole opened in front of her. She felt the touch of a cold wind. The ghost pulled at her dress. 'Quick! Quick, or it will be too late,' he said. In a moment, they had both disappeared into the hole.

CHAPTER 8

10

The Terrible Secret

When Virginia did not come down for tea, her mother sent someone to call her. But Virginia could not be found anywhere. At first, Mrs Otis was not alarmed. Virginia often went into the garden at this time to collect flowers for the dinner table. At six o'clock, however, she began to worry. She sent the boys outside to look for her daughter while she and her husband searched every room in the house.

At half past six, the boys returned. They had found no sign of their sister. The family were all now extremely worried. Mr Otis remembered the camp in Canterville park. A few days earlier he had given his permission for gypsies* to stay there. He called Washington and the Duke to walk to the park with him.

They found that the gypsies had left their camp quite suddenly. The fire was still burning. Mr Otis was sure that the travellers had taken his daughter. He sent men to all the police stations in the area. Then he called for his horse and rode away to look for Virginia in the next village. The Duke went with him.

On the way, they stopped at the railway station but there was no news of the missing girl. The next village was Bexley, a favourite place for gypsies to make camp. Mr Otis and the Duke searched all over the common land. But there was no sign of either the gypsies or Virginia. They even woke up the village policeman, but he could give them no information.

Tired and heartbroken, they rode back to Canterville Chase in the dark. At the end of the road, Washington and the twins were waiting for them with lamps. There was still no sign of Virginia. While they were away, Washington had even organised a search of the waters of the lake. The gypsies had been found in a village ten miles away. They said they had left Canterville in a hurry to go to a festival on the other side of the country. They were very sorry to hear about Virginia's disappearance. Four of them actually returned to help in the search.

Mr Otis heard all this news as they rode up to the house. There was nothing more they could do that night. Poor Mrs Otis was lying down in the library, almost mad with fear for her daughter. Mr Otis at once asked Mrs Umney to bring food. He made everyone eat something, but it was a sad, silent meal.

'We can't do any more tonight,' said Mr Otis. 'You must all go to bed now. Tomorrow morning, I'll ask Scotland Yard• for help.'

As they were leaving the room, they heard the clock sound midnight. Suddenly, there was a terrible noise of thunder and a loud crash. Strange, unearthly music filled the air. They looked up.

Part of the wall at the top of the stairs had opened. Virginia walked out. She was carrying a little box, and her face was white. In a moment they all ran up to her. Mrs Otis put her arms round the girl and the young Duke covered her face with kisses. The twins danced excitedly round the happy group.

'Where have you been, young woman?' asked Mr Otis angrily. He thought she had played a joke on them. 'The

• *Scotland Yard is the central office of the London police.*

Duke and I have been looking for you all over the country. You must never play these practical jokes any more.'

'We can play jokes on the ghost! On the ghost!' screamed the twins as they danced about.

'My dearest girl! Thank God you're safe. You must never leave my side again,' her mother said.

'Father, I've been with the ghost,' said Virginia. 'He's dead now, and you must come and see him. He was a very bad man, but he was really sorry at the end. He gave me this box of jewels* before he died.'

Everyone looked at her in shocked silence, but she was quite serious. She made a sign for them to follow her through the opening in the wall. They went into a hidden, secret part of the house. None of them had seen it before. Finally, they reached a great wooden door. When Virginia touched it, the heavy door opened slowly.

They walked into a little, low room with one small window. It was like a room in a prison. A skeleton lay on the floor. Its legs were chained to a large, metal ring in the stone wall. Just beyond the reach of the skeleton's hands lay a plate and a glass that had once held food and water...

The family looked in horror at the terrible secret Virginia had discovered. She was down on the floor beside the skeleton, her hands together and her mouth moving silently.

'Look!' said one of the twins. He had climbed up to the window to try to see which part of the house they were in. 'Look! That old, dead almond tree has flowers on it. I can see them clearly in the moonlight.'

'God has taken him,' said Virginia. Her eyes had a

The family looked in horror at the terrible secret Virginia had discovered.

beautiful light in them.

'How good and kind you are!' said the Duke. He put his arms round her and kissed her.

CHAPTER 9 11

The Garden of Death

Four days later, a funeral started from Canterville Chase at eleven o'clock at night. The carriage was pulled by eight black horses. Lord Canterville himself came from Wales and led the walkers behind the carriage. Next came the Otis family, followed by Mrs Umney. A hole in the ground was ready in the lonely garden near Canterville church. The little group collected there for the short service. At the last moment, Virginia stepped forward with a cross made of pink and white flowering almond branches. The moon covered her with a silver light and a nightingale began to sing. Then she remembered the ghost's description of the Garden of Death. On the way home, she cried quietly and did not speak a word.

The next morning, Mr Otis talked to Lord Canterville about the jewels given to Virginia by the ghost. 'It's quite clear to me, Lord Canterville, that these jewels belong to your family. My wife knows about jewels, and she says that they could be sold for a very high price. My daughter cannot possibly accept something so valuable. Such jewels may be necessary for the family of an English lord, but we Americans believe in the principles of hard work and a simple life. We have no need of such valuable things. I must ask you to take the jewels with you. Perhaps Virginia could just keep the pretty box in memory of Sir Simon.'

Lord Canterville listened politely and then took Mr Otis's hand. 'My dear Sir, your daughter did something very important for Sir Simon. My family and I admire her bravery. The jewels don't really belong to us. Until now, we didn't even know they existed. The jewels are obviously hers. And anyway, if I take them from her now, the ghost will surely return at once!'

Mr Otis tried to argue for a little longer, but Lord Canterville was firm. Virginia was able to keep the box and the jewels. When she married the Duke of Cheshire some time after, her marvellous jewels were much admired.

Later, the Duke and the new Duchess went down to Canterville Chase. They visited the lonely little garden of Canterville church and looked at the stone with Sir Simon's name on it. Virginia sat down on a wooden seat while her husband lay at her feet. He smoked a cigarette and looked up at her beautiful eyes.

Suddenly, he threw down the cigarette and took her hand. 'Virginia, a wife must have no secrets from her husband,' he said seriously.

She laughed. 'My dear! I have no secrets from you.'

'Yes, you have,' he answered. 'You've never told me what happened when you were locked up with the ghost.'

'Please don't ask me. I can't tell you. Poor Sir Simon! He taught me a lot. Yes, don't laugh, he really did! He made me see what Life is and what Death means. And he

'He made me see what Life is and what Death means.'

taught me that Love is stronger than both.'

The Duke stood up and kissed his wife. 'You can have your secret,' he said, 'if I can have your heart.'

'You have always had that,' said Virginia.

The Model Millionaire

He was not very clever, but he was very good-looking, with a fine profile and clear grey eyes.

The Model Millionaire 12

Unless a man is rich, it does not matter how charming* he is. Rich men may lead a romantic life, but not those without a profession. Poor men should be practical. It is better to have a permanent income* than to be a success in society. Hughie Erskine never realised how true this was in modern life. He was not very clever. He never said a brilliant thing or even an unkind one in his life. But he was very good-looking, with a fine profile* and clear grey eyes. He was as popular with men as he was with women. He was a good horseman, could shoot well and loved fishing. In fact, he had every talent except one. Although he had tried everything, he did not have the talent for earning money.

For six months, he worked in the tea business but he was not a successful salesman. He often forgot to write down orders and lost a lot of customers. Then he managed a wine shop, but soon became tired of it. He did not like working long hours when all his friends were enjoying the lazy lives of gentlemen. Fortunately, he had a kind aunt who gave him a little money every month. Except for that, he had nothing. He was just an attractive young man with a nice face and no profession.

To make things worse, he was in love with Laura Merton. Her father was an army officer, who had returned from service in India with a bad temper* and a weak stomach. Hughie and Laura were the best-looking young pair in London, but neither of them had any money. Although Colonel Merton liked Hughie, he would not let him marry his daughter.

'Get ten thousand pounds of your own and come back to me,' he told the young man. 'Then, we'll see.' Hughie was sad, but he and Laura continued to meet regularly.

▪■▪

One morning on his way to the Mertons' home, Hughie stopped to see his friend, Alan Trevor, who was a painter. Many people these days are painters - only a few are artists. Trevor was a strange, rough man with a long, untidy beard. But when he had a paintbrush in his hand, he was a true artist. Everyone wanted to buy his pictures.

At first, Trevor had liked Hughie for his easy manner and good looks. 'A painter only needs two kinds of people,' he used to say. 'He needs beautiful ones and stupid ones. It's good to look at beautiful people and easy to talk to stupid ones.' However, as time went on, he grew to like Hughie even more for his bright spirit and generous nature.

Trevor was just finishing a life-size portrait of a beggar* man. The beggar himself was standing in a corner of the studio. He was a thin, old man, with a face like crumpled* paper, and a very sad expression. A rough, brown coat was thrown across his back and his thick boots had holes in them. He held a stick* with one hand and with the other he held out a shabby* hat for money.

'What a wonderful old man!' Hughie said in his friend's ear. 'But he looks so very sad!'

'Of course he does,' said Trevor. 'You don't expect a beggar to look happy, do you?'

'How much do you pay him?' asked Hughie.

'A shilling• an hour.'

'And how much do you get for your pictures, Trevor?'

'Oh, for this I'll get two thousand pounds.'

Hughie laughed. 'Well, I don't think you pay him enough. He should get a percentage. He works as hard as you do.'

'Of course he doesn't,' said Trevor sharply. 'Painting is tiring work. There are moments when an artist can even demand the same respect as a man who works with his hands! Anyway, you mustn't talk, Hughie. I'm very busy. Smoke a cigarette and keep quiet.'

After some time, Trevor was called out of the studio for a few minutes. 'Don't run away,' he said. 'I'll be back in a moment.'

The beggar was thankful to sit down for a rest in a chair behind him. But he looked tired and sad. Hughie felt very sorry for* him. He searched his pockets for some money but could find only one piece of gold and a few pennies•.

'Poor old man,' he thought. 'He wants it more than I do. It'll mean no cabs* for two weeks. I'll have to walk everywhere.' He went across the room to the old man and put the gold piece into his hand.

The beggar was surprised. A little smile touched his dry, old mouth. 'Thank you, Sir,' he said. 'Thank you.'

Then Trevor returned. Hughie felt shy about his kind action and quickly said goodbye. He spent the day with

• *A shilling is pre-decimal British currency. Until 1971 there were 20 shillings in one pound and 12 pennies in one shilling.*

Hughie went across the room to the old man and put the gold piece in his hand.

Laura, who was a little angry with him. 'You don't have enough money to be so generous,' she said.

▪■▪

That evening, Hughie had to walk to his club. Alan Trevor was having a drink there so he sat down beside him.

'Well, Trevor, did you finish the picture?' he asked.

'All finished,' said Trevor. Then he looked closely at Hughie. 'What did you say to my old beggar man, this morning? He really seems to like you! He wanted to know your name and address. He also asked about your profession and the money you earn ... Of course, I had to tell him all about you...'

'The old beggar's probably waiting for me at home now!' laughed Hughie. 'But you're joking, Alan, aren't you? Poor old man. I wish I could do something for him. I think it's terrible that anyone could be so unhappy. I have a lot of old clothes at home. Do you think he could use them? His own clothes were full of holes.'

'But he looks wonderful in them,' said Trevor. 'I wouldn't want to paint him in a suit. You think he looks poor and unhappy, but to me he looks romantic. Anyway, I'll tell him what you said.'

'Trevor,' said Hughie seriously, 'you painters are all quite heartless.'

'Our business is to paint the world as it is, not to try to change it,' said his friend. 'Now, how's Laura? The old man was interested in her.'

'Did you tell him about her?' asked Hughie, greatly surprised.

'I certainly did,' replied Trevor. 'He now knows all about the Colonel's hard heart, his beautiful daughter and the ten thousand pounds.'

'You told that old beggar all about my private business?' said Hughie. He looked very red and angry.

Trevor laughed loudly. 'My dear Hughie, that "old beggar" is one of the richest men in Europe. He could easily buy all London tomorrow! He has a house in every important capital city in the world.'

'What do you mean?' asked Hughie.

'That old man in my studio today was Baron Hausberg. He's a great friend of mine - he buys all my pictures. A month ago, he asked me to paint him as a beggar, just for fun. It's the sort of fantasy that only a millionaire would have. And I must say, I think he looked marvellous in those old clothes.'

'Baron Hausberg!' said Hughie. 'And I gave him a gold piece!'

'You gave him money?' Trevor looked at him in disbelief. Then he gave a great shout of laughter. 'You'll never see it again.'

'Why didn't you tell me?' asked Hughie angrily. 'You let me do the wrong thing!'

'I didn't know you were so generous with your money, Hughie. I can understand you might want to kiss one of my pretty models ... but why would you give money to an ugly one? Anyway, at the time, I knew that Hausberg didn't want me to mention his name.'

'He must think I'm really stupid,' said Hughie.

'Not at all. He was in a very good mood after you left. He kept laughing to himself. I couldn't understand why he was so interested in you, but I see it all now. He'll use

'You gave him money?' Trevor looked at him in disbelief.

your money for you and pay you the interest every six months. And he'll have an excellent story to tell all his friends.'

'I am unlucky,' said Hughie crossly. 'The best thing I can do is go to bed. And you mustn't tell anyone, Trevor. I should never want to show my face in society again.'

'Don't worry about it, Hughie. After all, it only shows your kind and generous spirit. And don't run away. Have another cigarette and talk about Laura...'

But Hughie did not want to talk. He walked home still feeling very unhappy. He was sure everyone would soon know how stupid he had been.

▪ ■ ▪

The next morning at breakfast, an old gentleman arrived. 'I work for Baron Hausburg,' he announced. 'I wish to speak to Mr Erskine.'

Hughie held out his hand. 'I'm Erskine,' he said.

'I've come from Baron Hausberg, Mr Erskine-'

'Please tell the Baron I'm very sorry,' said Hughie uncertainly. 'I didn't know-'

The old gentleman smiled kindly. 'The Baron has asked me to bring you this letter. Will you open it?'

A message was written on the outside. It said, 'A present to Hugh Erskine and Laura Merton, from an old beggar.' Inside, there was a cheque for ten thousand pounds.

The young people were able to marry at once, and Baron Hausberg was there to give them his good wishes. So was Alan Trevor. He said in Hughie's ear, 'You don't often meet a millionaire model, but a model millionaire is even less common!'

The young people were able to marry at once.

The Sphinx without a Secret

Suddenly, I heard someone call my name.

The Sphinx without a Secret*

13

One afternoon, I was sitting outside a café in the heart of Paris, drinking a glass of wine. Until a few days before, I had been on holiday in the south of France. I had decided to stop in Paris on my way home to see a famous collection of French paintings. Now, I was enjoying a last evening in my favourite city, watching the crowds hurrying past in all their rich variety, some well dressed, others poor and shabby...

Suddenly, I heard someone call my name. I turned round and saw Lord Gerald Murchison. We had been at university together, but I had not seen him for ten years. I was very pleased to see him again and took his hand happily.

At Oxford, we had been very good friends. I had liked him very much. He was good-looking, with a kind nature and an honest character. We used to say that he was the best of men. His only fault, we joked, was that he always spoke the truth. But we secretly admired him for it.

I thought he had changed a lot. He now looked very worried and uncertain. The problem was probably a woman. 'Are you married yet, Gerald?' I asked.

'I don't understand women well enough,' he answered.

'My dear Gerald,' I said, 'we mustn't try to understand women! We must just love them.'

'I can't love if I don't understand,' he said unhappily.

So I had guessed right! 'I believe there's a mystery woman in your life, Gerald. Will you tell me about her?'

'Let's go for a walk,' replied Murchison. 'We'll find a quiet place for dinner. Then you can tell me what you have been doing all these years.'

'I want to hear about you, first,' I said. 'Tell me your mystery.'

He took a photograph out of his pocket and gave it to me without speaking. I looked at it and saw a tall, richly dressed woman with long hair. She had a distant look in her large, dark eyes.

'What do you think of that face?' asked Murchison. 'Is it the face of a woman who tells lies?'

I examined it carefully. It was the face of someone who had a secret. But I could not say if the secret was good or bad. The woman was not beautiful in the usual way. The little smile that touched her lips was not sweet, and it seemed to show some mystery in her character.

'Well,' said Murchison impatiently, 'what do you say?'

'I'll give you my opinion when you've told me all about her,' I said.

We had dinner together and talked of other things until coffee was brought. Then Lord Murchison lit a cigarette and told me his story.

■■■

One afternoon, he was walking down Bond Street• in London at about four o'clock. There was a lot of traffic moving very slowly. A little yellow carriage took his attention. Inside it, he saw the face of the woman in the

• *Bond Street is a street in central London famous for its expensive and exclusive shops.*

photograph. At once, Murchison felt an attraction to her. All that night and all the next day, he thought of her. He walked about the streets of London looking for her. But he could not find the lovely stranger.

About a week later, he was invited to visit some friends. Dinner was for eight o'clock but at half past eight, they were still waiting for the final guest. Finally, the door opened and a voice announced, 'Lady Alroy'. It was the woman from the yellow carriage.

She came slowly into the room, wearing a silver grey dress and looking like a thin finger of moonlight. Murchison was very pleased when he was asked to sit next to her at dinner.

'I think I saw you in Bond Street recently, Lady Alroy,' he said, after they had sat down.

Her face went white. 'Please don't talk so loudly. Someone might hear you,' she said in a low voice.

Murchison was afraid that he had made a bad start. He wondered why she was so nervous about being seen in Bond Street. At that time of day, it was a place where a lady could be seen, even in a carriage alone. Perhaps she had been on her way to meet a lover! But he pushed the thought away. She was a respectable lady with a position in society. Her place at this table tonight proved that. Such an idea was quite impossible. And yet...

He tried to interest her in other subjects. She spoke very little, and always in the same low, musical voice. He told me that he fell deeply, stupidly in love with her that evening. The air of mystery around her excited him.

Finally, the door opened and a voice announced, 'Lady Alroy'.

As she was leaving soon after dinner, he said, 'I hope I can see you again, Lady Alroy.' She did not answer at once, but looked around. No one was listening. Then she said, 'Yes, come to my house tomorrow at half-past four.'

When she had gone, Murchison asked the other guests about her. He learned that she was a widow* with a beautiful house in Park Lane. There seemed to be no mystery in her social life. She lived at one of the best addresses in London and was obviously a very rich woman.

The next day, Murchison arrived at exactly four thirty, but was told that Lady Alroy had gone out. He went unhappily to his club and wrote her a letter. He suggested another afternoon, but no answer came for several days. At last, he got a little note. 'Come on Sunday at four o'clock. Please do not write to me here again. I'll explain when I see you.'

On Sunday, she was kind and sweet to him. As he was leaving, she said, 'If you write to me again, send the letter to "Mrs Knox, Whittaker's Library, Green Street". I can't receive letters in my own home. There are good reasons why not...'

Murchison was worried by her unconventional behaviour. No respectable woman would use a secret address in a poor district of London.

All through the spring, Lord Murchison saw a lot of Lady Alroy, and the air of mystery was always with her. Sometimes, he thought she must be in the power of some man. Then he thought that was impossible – she was too much in control of herself. At last, he decided to ask her to marry him. He was tired of the secret visits and the secret letters.

She agreed to see him the following Monday. At the time, Murchison thought he was madly in love with her. The mystery just made him angry. Now, looking back, he understood that the mystery was the strongest part of her attraction.

'Oh, why did chance lead me to discover the truth?' he asked.

'So you discovered the truth, did you?' I said.

'I'm afraid I did,' Murchison said, and continued his story.

▪■▪

On the following Monday, he went out to lunch and at about four o'clock he took the shortest way back to his club. It led through some of the poorest and dirtiest streets in the city. Suddenly, Murchison saw Lady Alroy in front of him, with her face half covered. She was hurrying along the street, her head down.

Murchison's heart beat faster. A woman in Lady Alroy's social position could have no good reason for being in such a place ... and all alone! If she was meeting a secret lover, then he must be of the lowest class. But Murchison decided that he must know the truth.

When she came to the last house in the street, Lady Alroy took out a key. She opened the door and went inside.

'Here is the mystery,' Murchison said to himself. He hurried on and examined the house. It seemed to be the kind of place where people took rooms. Lady Alroy had dropped her handkerchief* outside. Murchison picked it up and put it in his pocket. After a few minutes' thought, he decided that it was not right to watch her secretly. So he continued on his way to the club.

Lady Alroy was hurrying along the street, her head down.

At six o'clock, he called at the house in Park Lane. Lady Alroy was pleased to see him. She was looking very lovely that evening. 'I'm so glad to see you,' she said. 'I haven't been out all day.'

Lord Murchison looked at her in great surprise. Then he pulled the handkerchief out of his pocket. 'You dropped this in Cumnor Street this afternoon, Lady Alroy,' he said calmly.

She looked at him in terror, but did not take the handkerchief. 'What were you doing there?' Murchison asked.

'Why are you questioning me?' she said.

'I love you,' he replied. 'I came here today to ask you to marry me.' Lady Alroy hid her face in her hands and started to cry.

'You must tell me,' Murchison said.

She stood up and looked straight at him. 'Lord Murchison, I was doing nothing that need trouble you,' she said.

'You went to meet someone, didn't you? This is your mystery!'

She went very white, and said, 'I went to meet no one.'

'That's not true,' Murchison shouted. He was mad with anger and said some terrible things to her.

'I'm not lying, Lord Murchison,' she replied.

Finally, he ran out of the house. Next day, Lady Alroy wrote him a letter, which he sent back unopened. Then he went away for a month to Norway with a friend.

'Lord Murchison, I was doing nothing that need trouble you,' she said.

When he came back, the first thing he saw in the *Morning Post*• was a report of the death of Lady Alroy. She had been taken ill suddenly and had died in five days. Murchison shut himself in his house and saw no one. He had loved her so much.

'Did you go to Cumnor Street, Gerald?' I asked. 'Did you go to the house?'

'Yes,' he answered, 'I went to the house. I had to go.' And he told me the rest of the story.

He knocked at the door of the house in Cumnor Street and a woman opened it. 'I'd like to take a room,' he said.

'Well, Sir,' she said, 'I have three empty rooms on the ground floor. They really belong to a lady, but I haven't seen her for three months and she hasn't paid me. You can have them, if you like.'

Murchison showed her the photograph. 'Is this the lady?'

'That's her, sure enough,' said the woman. 'When is she coming back?'

'The lady is dead,' he replied.

'Oh no!' said the woman. 'She was my very best client. She paid me three pounds just to sit in my rooms occasionally.'

'Did she meet someone here?' asked Murchison.

'No, Sir. No one. She always came alone.'

'What did she do here?' he asked.

'She just sat and read books, and sometimes had tea,' said the woman.

'I did not know what to say,' Murchison told me. 'I gave the woman some money and came away.' He

• *The* Morning Post *was a national daily newspaper*

looked at me. 'Now, you've heard the story. What did it all mean? Do you believe it was true?'

'Yes,' I said slowly, 'I do.'

'But why did Lady Alroy go there?'

'My dear Gerald,' I answered, 'Lady Alroy was a woman with a deep love of mystery. She took the rooms because she liked going there with her face covered. She enjoyed playing the part of a heroine in a romantic novel. But it was all in her head. Lady Alroy was, in fact, a Sphinx without a secret.'

'Do you really think she was?'

'I'm sure of it,' I replied.

He took the photograph from his pocket and looked at it for a long time.

'I wonder...?' he said at last.

EXERCISES

THE CANTERVILLE GHOST

A Choose the best way to complete each of these sentences - a, b, c or d.

1 Lord Canterville sold Canterville Chase because...

a ...he needed money.
b ...he preferred to live in London.
c ...his wife was frightened in the library.
d ...his family did not enjoy living in the house.

2 The Otis family shocked the ghost by...

a ...showing no fear of him.
b ...making strange noises at night.
c ...locking the library door.
d ...going to bed early.

3 The bloodstain in the library made the Otis family laugh because...

a ...Mrs Umney was frightened of it.
b ...it was a different colour every day.
c ...it disappeared in the morning.
d ...it moved around the room.

4 Mr Otis did not want Virginia to accept Sir Simon's jewels because...

a ...his wife did not like them.
b ...they were not very valuable.
c ...his daughter did not need them.
d ...he did not respect Lord Canterville.

B Answer these questions in your own words.

1 When did the bloodstain in the library at Canterville Chase first appear?
2 Why did the ghost very much want to appear in his own armour?
3 How had Sir Simon Canterville died?
4 What secret did Virginia keep from her husband?

C Choose the correct word or phrase to complete these sentences.

1 The twins ... for their bad behaviour.

a often beat **b** often beaten **c** were often beaten
d were often beat

2 Mr Otis and his sons found a large ... of old armour on the floor.

a dress **b** suit **c** suite **d** coat

3 'If I ever meet that bird, ... off its head.'

a I'd cut **b** I'll cut **c** I cut **d** I've cut

4 'Love is ... Death.'

a strong as **b** more strong than **c** stronger than
d more stronger than

D What differences were there in the ways the Otis family and the Canterville family behaved towards the ghost? Write 100-150 words describing the differences.

The Model Millionaire

A Are these sentences true or false? If you think that a sentence is false, give a reason.

1 Colonel Merton would not let his daughter marry Hughie Erskine because he did not like Hughie.
2 Hughie had to leave the tea business because he stole money.
3 A relation regularly gave Hughie money.
4 An old beggar was generous to Hughie and Laura.

B Answer these questions.

1 Why did Hughie not enjoy his job in the wine shop?
2 What did Colonel Merton tell Hughie to do?
3 Who was Alan Trevor?
4 Why was the beggar surprised when Hughie gave him money?

C In 100-150 words, write the 'excellent story' about Hughie Erskine that Baron Hausberg was able to tell his friends.

THE SPHINX WITHOUT A SECRET

A Choose the best way to complete these sentences - a, b, c or d.

1 Lady Alroy took rooms in Cumnor Street because she...

a ...was very rich.
b ...had a secret lover.
c ...wanted to be alone.
d ...enjoyed the idea of mystery.

2 Lord Murchison discovered Lady Alroy's secret rooms...

a ...at a dinner party.
b ...by chance.
c ...in a letter.
d ...from a newspaper story.

B Imagine you are Lady Alroy. Write (100-150 words) the letter you sent to Lord Murchison after his last visit to you.

GLOSSARY

armour *(n)* metal suit worn by fighting horsemen in medieval times

back home *(adv)* here, at home in the USA

beggar *(n)* person who asks for money in the street

bloodstain *(n)* mark where blood has been

butler *(n)* male domestic servant responsible, among other things, for serving drinks

butter *(n)* made from cream and eaten on bread; also used in cooking

cab *(n)* taxi

cap *(n)* small hat, often worn by female domestic workers

charming *(adv)* nice, with an attractive manner and conversation

common *(adv)* in the context of the English class system, *common* is used to mean vulgar or low born

crow *(v)* the noise a cock makes

crumpled *(adv)* if you make a piece of paper into a ball and then open it out, it is *crumpled*

feel sorry for someone *(v)* to feel someone is unlucky to be in the position they are in

footsteps *(pl n)* sound of feet walking

ghost *(n)* spirit of a dead person that returns to the living world

gypsy *(n)* *gypsies* are a travelling community with no permanent home

handkerchief *(n)* small square of cloth carried in the pocket

haunt *(v)* to visit or behave as a ghost*

hosepipe *(n)* flexible tube used to carry water to, for example, the garden or a fire

housekeeper *(n)* person employed to manage the domestic affairs of a house

humiliation *(n)* being made to look silly

income *(n)* the money you receive, either from work, investments or perhaps from a parent or other relative

jewels *(pl n)* valuable stones, often set in gold or silver

library *(n)* a room where books are kept

lightning *(n)* bright line of light in the sky produced during an electrical storm

mile *(n)* 1.6093 kilometres

model *(n)* a person who sits for an artist; *(adj)* excellent, without fault

pillow *(n)* you rest your head on a *pillow* when you sleep

portrait *(n)* a painting of a person, where the person is the main subject of the work

profile *(n)* the side view of the human face

recover *(v)* to get better

shabby *(adj)* in poor condition, for example clothes or furniture

shroud *(n)* a cloth, often white, used to cover a dead body

skeleton *(n)* hard parts of human body (bones)

Sphinx *(n)* the *Sphinx* is a figure from Egyptian sculpture and Greek mythology, a monster with a woman's head and a lion's body; used metaphorically to mean a person of mystery

stain *(n)* an unwanted permanent mark (see bloodstain*)

starve *(v)* to die for want of food

stick *(n)* long, thin piece of wood

temper *(n)* someone's general mood

thunder *(n)* loud crash heard during electrical storm; thunder follows lightning*

twins *(pl n)* two babies born at the same time; they may or may not be identical

widow *(n)* a married woman whose husband has died

wit *(n)* clever use of imagination and understanding; clever use of words to make people laugh

Richmond
58 St Aldates
Oxford
OX1 1ST
United Kingdom

Publishing Director: Sarah Thorpe
Managing Editor: Tanya Whatling
Editor: Jane Holt

Cover Illustration: Tim Gaudion
Illustrations: Andy Walker
Recording: Maria Jeanette Christiansen, Mauri Corretjé
Impressão: Reproset
Lote: 278565

Dados Internacionais de Catalogação na Publicação (CIP)
(Câmara Brasileira do Livro, SP, Brasil)

Wilde, Oscar, 1854-1900.
The Canterville ghost and other stories / Oscar Wilde. -- 1. ed. -- São Paulo : Moderna, 2019. -- (Richmond readers)

1. Contos irlandeses I. Título. II. Série.

19-23221 CDD-Ir823

Índices para catálogo sistemático:
1. Contos : Literatura irlandesa Ir823

Maria Alice Ferreira - Bibliotecária - CRB-8/7964

ISBN: 978-85-16-11726-9

Richmond
EDITORA MODERNA LTDA.
Rua Padre Adelino, 758 – Belenzinho
São Paulo – SP – Brasil – CEP 03303-904
www.richmond.com.br
2019
Printed in Brazil